LIVER

The Felix Pollak Prize in Poetry

The University of Wisconsin Press Poetry Series
Ronald Wallace, General Editor

LIVER

Charles Harper Webb

The University of Wisconsin Press

The University of Wisconsin Press
2537 Daniels Street
Madison, Wisconsin 53718

3 Henrietta Street
London WC2E 8LU, England

Printed in the United States of America

Library of Congress Cataloging-in-Publication Data

Webb, Charles Harper
Liver / Charles Harper Webb
116 pp.   cm. — (Felix Pollak prize in poetry)
ISBN 0-299-16570-1 (cloth: alk. paper)
ISBN 0-299-16574-4 (pbk: alk. paper)
I. Title. II. Series: Felix Pollak prize in poetry (Series)
PS3573.E194 L58 1999
811'.54—dc21   99-6457

for Karen

Contents

Acknowledgments

I would like to thank the editors of the following publications for first publishing these poems, sometimes in another version:

5 A.M.: "Trust"

AMERICAN POETRY REVIEW: "The Age of Orange": A History Inferred from Sentences in the *Oxford English Dictionary*

BAKUNIN: "Gifts"

CHATAHOOCHEE REVIEW: "Von Osten, His Teacher, Speaks of Clever Hans," "Legacy"

CHELSEA: "Beachcomber Hotel, Papeete," "Lost Lives," "Chapel in the Pines"

FREE LUNCH: "Mother Asleep"

GREENSBORO REVIEW: "Heart," "Prozac," "Towel Boy"

HARVARD REVIEW: "Someone Else's Good News"

THE JOURNAL: "Poem on My Anniversary," *"Over the Town"*

LAUREL REVIEW: "Rumpelstiltskin Convention," "Cherubs," "Myopia"

MADISON REVIEW: "George"

MICHIGAN QUARTERLY REVIEW: "Identifying with the Buddha"

NEBO: "Byron, Keats, and Shelley"

PARIS REVIEW: "Tone of Voice," "Coach Class Seats"

PLUM REVIEW: "Scarcity"

POET LORE: "Photo Titled 'Birth'"

POETRY EAST: "Musk Turtle"

POETRY FLASH: "Confidence"

POETRY INTERNATIONAL: "Floating Loin," "Love Poetry"

PLOUGHSHARES: "Wedding Dress," "Biblical Also-Rans"

PRESS: "Lampwick," "The Lighthearted Story of a Young Girl Raised by Trolls," "It's Good That Old People Get Crotchety"

SEATTLE REVIEW: "Munchausen's Syndrome"

SOUTH COAST POETRY JOURNAL: "Watch for Deer"

SOUTHERN POETRY REVIEW: "The Weight of Knowledge"

STEAM TICKET: "Losing My Hair"

SYCAMORE REVIEW: "Stegosaurus," "'Octopus,'" "Tenderness in Men"

TAMPA REVIEW: "At Summer's End," "The Function of Poetry"

WITNESS: "The Secret History of Rock & Roll"

YELLOW SILK: "Inheritance"

"Tarantula" first appeared in *The Faber Book of Movie Verse*, Faber and Faber, 1993

"Persistence of Sound," "Liver," and "Descent" first appeared in *Verse and Universe*, Milkweed Press, 1998

"Floating Loin," "Gifts," and "Love Poetry" were collected in the chapbook *Dr. Invisible and Mr. Hide*, published by Pearl Editions.

"Watch for Deer" won the *South Coast Poetry Journal* Competition in Poetry.

"Towel Boy" received the *Greensboro Review* Literary Award in Poetry.

The writing of this book was partially funded by California State University, Long Beach, Scholarly and Creative Activities Awards.

Special thanks to Ron Koertge, Walter Pavlich, Richard Garcia, Dinah Berland, and Judith Taylor for invaluable editorial assistance, and to Edward Hirsch, for whose support and example I'm more grateful than I can say.

Part I

Wedding Dress

She wants it and she doesn't want it: the lace neck
and sleeves, the waist so tight she'll need it refitted
the day before *the* day. She wants and doesn't want
the pleats and puffs and bows, the veil's force field
guarding her face, the train's long barge dragging behind,
the whole creation so elaborate she must be lowered
into it—like a knight onto his horse—with a crane.

She wants and doesn't want to choose her neckline:
Bertha, bateau, jewel, Queen Anne, decolletage;
her sleeves: *bishop, balloon, pouf, gauntlet, mutton leg;*
her silhouette: *ballgown, basque, empire, sheath, mermaid;*
her headpiece: *pillbox, derby, wreath, tiara, garden hat.*
She wants and doesn't want the four-page guest list,
the country club that overlooks the valley

like Indian scouts planning a surprise attack.
She wants and doesn't want the tryptich invitations,
the florist/psychic who intones, "I envision one black
vase per table, each holding a single white rose."
"I love him," she thinks, "but my Zeppelin tapes are melting;
my Bowie posters curling into flame. I love him,
but Uni High is vanishing like our senior *Brigadoon.*

I love him but my friends are turning into toasters,
china place settings, crystal salad bowls."
She wants and doesn't want the plane door closing,
Tahiti rushing toward her, then dropping behind,
Mom in her fuscia gown starting to stoop,
Dad giving her away as white hair falls: a fairy ring
around his feet. Even as she pays for it, her dress

is yellowing, the wedding pictures aging into artifacts,
her children staring at strangers: one in a penguin suit,
one in her glory. They can't believe that living
works this way—just as the boy can't believe what else
his pecker will be for; the girl, where babies grow,
how they get there, what every month will leak from her.
"I want it, but I don't want it," she'll say.

The Weight of Knowledge

At first you barely feel it—"Mama," "Da-Da,"
"Poo-poo"—light as the few hairs on your head.
Each week brings more: name, age, birthday,
control of body functions, the magic of "No!"

Facts cling to you, sticky-sweet as jujubes:
the laws of grammar and balancing on two feet;
the way a stone feels; how to throw it;
what it does to a hamster, and a glass tray.

Learning grasps your bones and pulls:
I before *e* except after *c*. Three times three
is nine. Field grounders on the short hop.
If teenagers yell "Hey kid!" at you, run.

Information pumps your muscles up:
secrets of the hypotenuse and quadratic
equation; how to drive a car and get a date;
what hormones are, and what they mean to you.

Knowledge pours in: the theme of "Lycidas";
definitions of *entropy* and *spirochete*;
how deep to bury a dead dog. Abstractions—
justice, social interest, love —weigh you down

like rolls of fat, along with the urologist's
phone number, the lawyer's fee, atrocities
of the Khmer Rouge and CIA, the real reasons
your wife married you. You're mountainous by now:

a freak, out of control. Walled in by books,
crushed by printouts, all circuits on overload—
not only can't you leave your room;
you couldn't get out of bed if you wanted to.

The Lighthearted Story of a Young Girl Raised by Trolls

—from an ad for Bournonville's "A Folk Tale"

Because the story is lighthearted, it doesn't tell
how the girl's stepmother left her to die. It skips over
how the trolls found her crying in the woods, hung her
by her feet like a dead deer, carried her squealing
to their cave, and would have eaten her except she was so thin.

It doesn't dwell on the darkness of the cave, the cold,
the beatings, her fear of the snaking mine, the cork-
tight crevices the trolls forced her to probe, the meat
they made her gag down raw, torn from carcasses
they butchered with their teeth. Grind or be ground down

was the rule for trolls and humans in that time before
child labor laws—time of plague and pox and purgatives,
when any scratch could kill, when few women survived
their childbearing years, and everyone who lived
did so in pain. Because the story is lighthearted,

we don't hear of the girl cowering at night, waiting
for the carrion-breath, the stony hands, the short,
thick organs like wood blocks ripping her. In those days,
when man was to wife as God to man, people
raped or killed their slaves at will; but because this story

is lighthearted, the trolls are cuddly humanists
charmed by the girl's gold hair and sapphire eyes,
her singing as she sweeps their cave, the way she mends
the furs they wear, taps holes in stone to let in light and air
adorns their plank table with eglantine and heather.

They weep when a young king on horseback finds the girl
deep in the woods, gathering herbs to spice their stew.
Still, they know she will remember them with love
in her palace with her silk gowns, ladies-in-waiting,
royal husband who worships her. (Because the story

is lighthearted, we don't hear how, nights, she screams
and cringes when the good king comes.) Famed
for their greed, the trolls place on her slender neck a rope
of diamonds the size of hens' eggs, and wave as she rides off
on the king's stallion, selfless tears in every eye.

Myopia

After they scalped my family, the Cheyennes
might have spared me for the way I seized
a rolling pin and tried to fight—unless
they knew I thought *they* were my family,
the burning wagons just our campfire flaring up.
They would have called me Sees-Things-as-a-Blur.

My eyes taught me humility: Pee Wee
batting champ one year; the next, too blind
to see the ball. Leaving the doctor's wearing
"flesh-tone" glasses (so no one would call me
Four-eyes), I shrilled, "Everything's so bright!"
Trees were limbs and leaves, not smudged green blobs.

Roofs and sky didn't meld into one gray.
Our Ford wasn't a blue fog that swallowed me.
Easy to understand a frontier boy shooting
a man to steal his "specs." Without them,
what could that boy be? A hunter who starved.
A farmer who could only see his land by lying on it.

Myopia is like a bad phone connection,
a TV with no antenna, an accent I can't
quite understand. It's like algebra to the kids
I tutor: fuzzy concepts fading into mist.
Hard to believe it's just light beams crossing
too soon, the image perfect, but not focused

on the screen. Watching dusk fade, I pray
the magic in my glasses stays.
I place them on a shrine beside my bed.
My lenses which art from heaven . . .
"Is this better, or this?" asks my optometrist.
It's hard to say. Without glasses,

the world seems watercolored by Monet.
I make things disappear for fun,
or when they hurt to see. Removing
my glasses helps ease me into dreams.
Someday my failing sight will lower me
like a rope ladder toward death's dark lake,
leaving just a few inches to fall.

Over the Town

Chagall looks thrilled to be sporting his best green shirt,
holding his wife Bella in the cross-chest carry as they swim
above the red, green, and gray Russian town, Vitebsk.
I held Connie, my first girlfriend, that way as we practiced life-

saving in the class where we met, both of us 15. Come Fall,
she dumped me for a senior; still, while they lasted, our days
seemed to float, changeless as stars in the June sky (though Physics
swore the stars were rocketing away.) While other artists moped,

look how happy Chagall is to be, in *Birthday*, an armless,
flying worm-man—a green-shirted, floating eel-man twisting
around from behind to kiss Bella, who holds a red, yellow, blue,
and white bouquet. He painted *Birthday* after Bella visited

on his, and made him feel above paltry physical laws.
Unthinkable not to be able to float, at any time, to Bella's lips.
Inconceivable that in 1944, "unexpectedly," the museum notes say
(how could a man in love ever expect such catastrophe?),

Bella would die, and change love's timeless present into
the past people mourn, not comprehending how happiness
concrete as a mountain could just disappear. Years in the future,
today will be part of my Golden Age. And yesterday,

with its hot blueberry bagels, its cuddling as we watched
Cemetary Man. I swear I'll never let it lump in with "the past,"
the way my years at home have bunched into "when I was a boy,"
and not events countless as the stars above pre-smog Houston:

the same stars Chagall and Bella loved over Vitebsk.
Standing in the very room where a painter named Gerbil
puked cherry jello to protest Art's sterility, I pick your pink-
and-blue-flowered dress out of the crowd, walk up behind you,

smooth your chestnut hair, then lean around (feet stuck like magnets
to the floor) and kiss you. I fold my arms around you in the cross-
chest carry and, mentally at least, lift you as if to float forever
high over L.A. As if I, mortal myself, could save your life.

Biblical Also-Rans

Hanoch, Pallu, Hezron, Carmi,
Jemuel, Ohad, Zohar, Shuni:
one Genesis mention's all you got.

Ziphion, Muppim, Arodi: lost
in a list even the most devout skip over
like small towns on the road to L.A.

How tall were you, Shillim?
What was your favorite color, Ard?
Did you love your wife, Iob?

Not even her name survives.
Adam, Eve, Abel, Cain—
these are the stars crowds surge to see.

Each hour thousands of Josephs,
Jacobs, Benjamins are born.
How many Oholibamahs? How many

Mizzahs draw first breath today?
Gatam, Kenaz, Reuel? Sidemen
in the band. Waiters who bring

the Perignon and dissappear.
Yet they loved dawn's garnet light
as much as Moses did. They drank

wine with as much delight.
I thought my life would line me up
with Samuel, Isaac, Joshua.

Instead I stand with Basemath, Hoglah,
Ammihud. Theirs are the names
I honor; theirs, the deaths I feel,

their children's tears loud as any
on the corpse of Abraham, their smiles
as missed, the earth as desolate

without them: Pebbles on a hill.
Crumbs carried off by ants.
Jeush. Dishan. Nahath. Shammah.

Persistence of Sound

A word is dead
When it is said,
Some say.
—*Emily Dickinson*

Some scientists say sound doesn't die.
It fades from hearing, but keeps rolling up
and down—smaller and smaller waves—forever.
Churchill orating, "We will never surrender,"
Nixon whining, "I am not a crook,"
Caruso singing *Vesti la giubba*—
the right machine might amplify the air-
squiggles their voices made, and pluck them
like worms from a wriggling pot.

I'd love to hear my dad ask Mom to marry him.
What did they sound like, conceiving me?
(Dad yelled, Mom whimpered, is my guess;
I'd love to be surprised.) I'd love to hear
Demosthenes's Greek, and the first Indo-European,
and what those Caucasians spoke
who left their perfect mummies in Xianping.

Anthropologists could hear the first human
step onto North America, and know,
by plotting sound decay, just when that was.
The air could prove a treasure trove dwarfing
Pompeii (Vesuvius still thundering;
Romans shrieking, burned alive.) Still, I hope

15

some sounds didn't survive: "You poison me!"—
"I picture Kevin when I come with you!"—
the slam of your door as I left for the last time.

I'd miss the softened tones of memory:
your laugh retained the way a gold
bracelet torn by a Viking off an Irish
arm and melted down, retains traces
of serpent form, and the soft, freckled skin
that warmed it, that the girl passed down to me—
the way a pterosaur's atoms (returned
to earth, reused over and over) retain
in their vibrations every fish it ate,
the squawks it made feeding its young,
the splash when its heart—so like mine—
stopped, and it dropped into the undulating sea.

Musk Turtle

While his relatives the red-ear sliders,
scripta elegans, glide gracefully,
or dart, their green-and-yellow legs a blur,

he humps across slimed bottom gravel:
bonsai hippo; unwitting clown of the aquarium.
Even his name is ignominy:

sternotherus odoratus, "stinkpot musk."
A living id, he mounts male red-ears twice
his size, and clings—dwarf bronco rider;

Old Man of the Sea. At feeding time,
the red-ears splash and bully, webbed feet
in his face, shoving him down. He paws the water

like a drowning man, lacking the spirit
to fight back, to seize an elegant
striped leg in his knife-jaws. The rare times

he breaks through the mob, he can't catch
bloodworm pellets as they do. His mouth gapes:
a clumsy fielder's glove. He lunges,

drops the ball, then sinks to the bottom to skulk,
and scavenge what slips by. None of his kind
will ever crawl through steaming forests

after rain, feasting on dewberries and soft
grubs like the box turtle, or glide through blue-green
waters over coral like the hawksbill,

or squat like the alligator snapper underneath
a rotten stump, ready to slice
some silver darter, drag some blithe duckling

down. Yet when beautiful things die—
the frilly koi, the leopard frog, the black-
spotted newt, the red-ear slider—it's the musk

turtle who cleans the mess their beauty leaves—
whose wide mouth opens to accept, whose tongue,
shaped like a soft, pink heart, enfolds them all.

Heart

Plato believed soul and intelligence lived there.
      Who wouldn't choose red, pulsing muscle
            Over gray spongecake-and-jelly in the head?

Who'd name a king Richard the Lion-Brained,
      Even if he was? Who'd trade kisses for candy
            In a brain-shaped box (although the heart—

Strange, veined tuber—needs lovers' eyes to shape it
      Like a woman's hips). "She broke my heart,"
            Someone sighs, and we know just what he means.

Months after Billy Hanson's dad "dropped dead,"
      I expected mine to fall, attacked
            By killer Valentines. What I recall

So well that it seems carved into my bones—
      The "Now I lay me down to sleep," my first
            Address and phone number, the softness

Of my mother's hand, the murmur of Brahms' lullaby
      As she soothed me against her breast
            Where I could hear the steady *badump, badump*—

I know these things are chemically laid down
      Among cerebral dendrites. Still, I don't say
            I know them by brain, but by heart.

Von Osten, His Teacher,
Speaks of Clever Hans

*Of the learned animals which fascinated Europe in the early twentieth century,
the most celebrated was the German horse, Clever Hans.*
—from Psychological Studies, *Carl. M. Chester*

Hans, add thirty-eight to twenty-three.
His left hoof taps six; his right, one: sixty-one.
Hans, on what day of the week
did June 12, 1900, fall? Two taps: Monday.
A circus owner, a physiologist,
a veterinarian, a psychologist,
the Director of the Berlin Zoo—each saw Hans
tell time from a watch, read and obey
written commands, resolve harmonic dissonance.
Each tested Hans himself, and left amazed
as I am always, Hans's nose nuzzling my hair.

Then the researcher Pfungst, using blinders,
kept Hans from seeing his examiners.
My poor pupil tapped at random, then reared
and kicked at Pfungst, who concluded that he—
Hans—detects eye shifts, tilts of the beard,
changes in breathing too slight for us to see.
When Hans has tapped enough, the testers' eyes
relax, breath slows, heads raise without our realizing it,
and Hans stops tapping. Herr Pfungst claims
that Hans's "learning" is a mere wish for carrots,

his reward for being right. Sceptics say the same
of virtue: "Good" men merely hope to merit
heaven—full oat sacks, eternally shod hooves.

What did Pfungst prove?
That a bright man can explain a clever beast.
That Hans cares enough to note our every move.
That, like us all, he tries to please.
That the species aren't forever separate,
like earth's north and south poles—
like light, which never in the whole
of time can catch up to itself. That, just
as Physics leaps from star to star across
heaven, something leaps across the space between us.
Leaden, hopeless families see my clever horse
and leave smiling, drunk on the unknown.

Tone of Voice

It pinks the cheeks of speech, or flushes the forehead.
It's a spring breeze in which words play, a scorching sun
that burns them red, slate clouds that cover them in ice.
Mastering tone, the child outgrows his sticks and stones.

"*Okay,*" he sneers, twisting the word in Mommie's eye.
Elipses, dashes, all capitals, underlines—
these are tuna nets through which tone's minnows slide.
"I love you" may arrive spiked like a mace, or snickering.

"State your name" from lawyers' lips can mean "You lie!"
Tone leaks the truth despite our best efforts to hide.
It's verbal garlic; mistress on a husband's hands.
Consider, dear, when you ask, "Where are my French fries?"

how you may stand in a silk teddy holding grapes,
a suit of mail holding a lance, a hangman's hood holding
a rope. As useless to protest, "I didn't mean that,"
as to tell a corpse, "Stand up. You misinterpreted my car."

Beachcomber Hotel, Papeete

While Katie crashes after our nine-hour flight,
I slip outside to watch dawn turn up the lights
on the land of grass skirts, bare breasts, and Gauguin.

Palms spread their fronds like emerald tailfeathers.
The "gray" lagoon, when I walk up, is clear
except for indigo flashes of fish. Beyond

a white collar of surf, Moorea jags from the slate sea.
Weeks after Kate and he broke up, a guy named Tim
kept driving by my house. I swore I'd shoot him

at the time, but watching mynah pairs chase tree to tree—
whinnying, clicking, screaming *waw-waw-waw*,
I pity how he cried (Kate says) and popped Prozac

after losing her. He's like the lone, black-crested bird
that whimpers as it pokes through red hibiscus—hapless
as the Tahitians who emerge to sweep and water

in fruit-basket hats and green flourescent shirts.
"Tim lacked ambition. And determination. And perseverance,"
Katie says. He faked a college degree, and claimed

to work in the "film industry" when he drove truck
for Blockbuster Video. Still, she took a year
to drop him, and another year to let him fall.

As we jostled like rowboats trying to link up in a hurricane,
I sometimes wondered if male and female, uncoerced
by church and state, can pull together over the long haul.

One night I screamed, "Tim's won! You're his revenge
on me." But that was in L.A., where it's chic
to scorn affirming, and to call despair "integrity."

Here in Tahiti, wedding vows fresh in my ears,
I affirm, on pain of emotional bankruptcy, my marriage
and my wife. I affirm my ambition to love,

my determination to love, my perseverance in loving.
In the tear-stained face of hopelessness, the yawning
face of ennui, the sneering, post-modern face of contempt,

I trumpet "Kate and Me!" and hack an oyster—a pearl
oyster—straight into Death's jaundiced eye as a pale
girl I'll never know glides, nude, across the hotel pool.

Like a soft breeze, she breaks the sapphire surface
into waves that pulse and shimmer as the sun
pulls itself, dripping, out of the gold sea.

Floating Loin

This is a very pretty throw, and quite well suited to the supple frame of youth.
—E. J. Harrison, *Junior Judo*

Eight-year-olds didn't tote Uzis in 1959; they wouldn't tong out
both your eyeballs for a dime. But there was still the blur of fists
to fear, blood in your mouth, shoes in your ribs, the hard weight
of a ninth grader on your chest, and afterwards the long walk home,
the jeered "got his ass kicked," friends shrinking back
as if you'd give them polio. In self defense, I stole *Junior Judo*

from the library. In my backyard behind the pines
where Mom couldn't see and scream us in with prophecies
of compound fractures and iron lungs, Joey West and I practiced
okuriashibarai, "sweeping ankle throw," *ouchigari*, "major inner reaping,"
taiotoshi, "the body drop," *ukigoshi*, the "floating loin."
We pushed, tugged, flopped, flailed, failed to send each other

flying as Bob Constable down the street whispered of a place
on White Oak Bayou where, hidden by mulberry trees,
boys wrestled naked, and the winner got to "put his peter in
the loser's butt." I pictured my small weenie between stinking buns,
and saw one more of life's incomprehensible humiliations,
one more need for judo. Six years later, Bob was "rolling queers":

stealing their wallets; beating them with chains. Joey and I
had stopped being friends, but Kenny Sullivan and I paid cash
for two months of karate after Mike Todd—six-six, two-eighty,
who later wrestled as Mike the Big 'Un—dragged Kenny
by his jock around the Jones High track. In our first lesson,
Sensei Halliburton kicked a boy in the face, and dropped him,

spewing blood, out cold. "The dumb shit moved," *Sensei* snarled.
"Come on, you pussy—up!" I left without my money back—
money Dad gave me for a National Honor Society pin.
But no Golden Torch of Learning on my lapel could have stopped
Lonnie Wayne from slamming me against a steel locker,
spewing halitosis in my face while my first girlfriend, Sherry James,

wailed, "Don't hurt him, Lonnie. I'll go back with you!"
I still dream of dropping Lonnie with an *uchimata*, "inner thigh throw,"
or hoisting him above my head in *katagumura*, "the shoulder wheel,"
or *seoinage*, "a very violent shoulder throw which can often
be successfully applied by a short judoka to a taller one."
I should at least have tried a floating loin: the only throw I ever

brought off perfectly. Day after day, Joey and I had twisted
and contorted like the boys in *Junior Judo*, pressed so close
we'd have felt queer if we'd known what queer was. When tall,
skinny teenager Ben Brandt, who now owns Brandt's Auto Supply,
found us knee-deep in White Oak Bayou, catching crawdads,
he chased us with an ax, bellowing, "I'll chop your balls off!"

Mom was hanging clothes when we exploded from the woods.
Ben stopped in the charred spot where Dad burned leaves
as we clawed over the fence. "You little queers," Ben yelled,
"go suck your momma's sugar tit," then disappeared,
a sulphur shame-cloud where he'd been. We practiced judo
daily for a week until somehow my arm caught Joey's waist just right,

I got my body under his, and flexed my knees, and lifted him
onto my hip, over and down onto his back: a floating loin so hard
his breath gushed out in a loud "Whoof!" and he lay gasping
like a catfish in a sack. I knew, that instant, how *Sensei* would feel,
his student bleeding at his feet—and Bob, and Mike, and Lonnie Wayne.
I knew why the strong despise the weak. Why Auschwitz, My Lai,

Tien an Men Square had to be. Why mercy is divine, and not to be
hoped for. I loathed Joey's red face and gasping mouth
and panicked eyes even as, stiffening, I intoned "I'm sorry,"
until he caught a breath like a rag rope and pulled himself painfully,
hand-over-hand, across death's parapet back onto solid ground,
and stood shakily, and stumbled home, afraid to look at me.

Tenderness in Men

It's like plum custard at the heart of a steel girder,
cool malted milk in a hot bowling ball.

It's glimpsed sometimes when a man pats a puppy.
If his wife moves softly, it may flutter like a hermit thrush

into the bedroom, and pipe its pure, warbling tune.
Comment, though, and it's a moray jerking back into its cave.

Dad taught me to hide tenderness like my "tallywhacker"—
not to want or accept it from other men. All I can do

for a friend in agony is turn my eyes and, pretending
to clap him on the back, brace up his carapace with mine.

So, when you lean across the table and extend your hand,
your brown eyes wanting only good for me, it's no wonder

my own eyes glow and swell too big for their sockets
as, in my brain, dry gulleys start to flow.

Towel Boy

My leg bones had grown at different rates,
hobbling me when I tried to run,
so when the ROTC commander,
Captain Fleck, who looked a little
like my dad in his army uniform,
marched into gym class my first day
of high school, and said I could be
on the rifle team, I joined. Gym
as a "nonparticipant," I knew, meant
I'd wind up a towel boy, tossing
small, rough, white towels that stank
of lye to a line of sweating, swearing,
hooting boys who snapped each others'
hairy butts, every one sure he was
better than me because he was buck naked
after a workout, and I—poor cripple
who'd never dunk a ball or fuck a girl—
was serving him. I knew from seeing
towel boys in junior high that, no matter
how hard I didn't stare, no matter how
contemptuously I tossed the cotton
squares, I would look queer facing
that menagerie of elephants and anteaters,
those sets of balls like bearded,
mismatched chins. What could I do
except report to ROTC the next day?
I hoped for a John Wayne film: brave
recruits with faces full of character—
a little green, but ready, with the right

On August 28, 1963, over 200,000
Negroes and whites, led by Reverend
Martin Luther King, Jr., marched for
civil rights in Washington. On August
30, a "hot line" was completed between
Washington and Moscow. On August
31, AFL-CIO President George Meany
proposed a 35-hour work week. On
September 6, Governor George Wallace
used state troopers to block integration of
four white schools in Huntsville,
Alabama. On September 7, students
demonstrated in Saigon against U.S.
support of the Diem government. On
September 8, Jack Nicklaus won the
World Series of Golf. On September 9,
President John F. Kennedy denied plans-
by the CIA to intervene in Vietnam and
stopped the draft for married men. On the
same day, the first Negroes attended pre-
viously all-white Alabama public
schools. On September 11, Senator
Barry Goldwater accused the Kennedy
administration of trying to turn the U.S.
into "a socialized welfare state." On
September 12, President Kennedy said he
would not approve a plan to bus children
out of their neighborhoods. On September
13, Kennedy urged "full consideration" to

training, to slaughter Krauts and Japs and ride through liberated towns in tanks, while cheering French sex kittens blew kisses and more. Instead I saw a mob of four-eyed geeks and limping pizzaheads like me. Dwarfish beachballs, tall stringbeans—every misfit at Simmons High was here. Lieutenant Jones— Ichabod Crane in fatigues—broke us into squads and platoons as student corporals passed out khaki uniforms with brass buttons and buckles that, instead of practicing marksmanship, judo, survival skills, we spent our first week polishing. My platoon sergeant, a fat senior named Schmickel, whose body shuddered when he walked, called me "Soldier" in a croak that sounded like he hawked esophagus up with the spit that misted me with each command. The first day I wore my uniform to school, even my best friends— Johnny Sullivan, Dave Inman, Stevie Wendell—shied away. Teddi Walker, who'd flirted with me all 9th grade, and who I dreamed of asking out once I could drive, sneered, "Why d'you want to be a dumb Rot-see?" I got two demerits that day: one for shoes, and one for belt buckle. Neither gleamed bright enough for Schmickel, who marched us up and down the parking lot, grunting

the hiring of the mentally retarded. On September 15, a bomb exploded at a Negro church in Birmingham, Alabama, killing four children, injuring many more. On September 17, the House authorized $175 million to build fallout shelters. On September 20, President Kennedy proposed a joint U.S.–Soviet manned expedition to the moon. On September 25, the Supreme Soviet ratified the limited nuclear test ban treaty. On September 26, a British high court found no evidenceof security "leakage" due to the affair between War Minister Lord John Profumo with call girl Christine Keeler, despite her link to Russian spy Evgeny "Honeybear" Ivanov. On September 27, Joseph Valachi described "La Cosa Nostra" to the Senate Permanent Investigations Subcommittee. On October 2, Defense Secretary McNamara and General Maxwell Taylor stated that the U.S. military task in Vietnam should be completed by late 1965. On October 5, South Vietnamese police beat three U.S. journalists who witnessed the self-immolation of a Buddhist monk. On October 6, the Dodgers swept the Yankees in four straight games to win the World Series. On October 7, the British film Tom Jones opened in New York. On

"Hut, hut, hut," and "A-ten-HUT!"
as if he were being punched in his fat gut.
I got another demerit for yelling "Don't
yell at me," and another for not adding
"Sir." The next day I got "written up"
when someone saw me sneak past
the flag without saluting. There were no
friends in Rot-see, only spies. My rifle,
when I got one, lacked a firing pin;
its riflings had been worn away by years
of cleaning. I'd had my own Savage
.22 since I turned ten, and could knock
a crow off a fence at a hundred yards,
but scored a demerit for not cleaning
my gun (which had never been shot
and never would be) well enough,
another one for calling it a "gun,"
and two more for telling Schmickel,
"That's no rifle; it's a damn smoothbore!"
Minutes later, I tacked on one more
for calling him "Schmuckel" to the Kallikak
beside me, who as soon as I walked away,
told. As a private, I couldn't march right up
to Captain Fleck and speak. I had to
relay questions through Lieutenant Jones,
via Schmickel; so it was a week before
the Captain's answer to my question
trickled down: I couldn't join the rifle
team until I'd "logged a year of duty."
"Fleck lied to me," I told Dad.
"My friends are right. Rot-sees are geeks
and idiots." "Don't be a quitter,"

October 9, President Kennedy announced
plans to sell Russia $250 million worth of
wheat. Former Vice President Nixon
called the deal "this administration's
biggest mistake." On October 13,
Jacqueline Kennedy returned from touring
the Aegean on a yacht owned by Greek
tycoon Aristotle Onassis. On October
14, the U.S. Supreme Court directed
Florida to review the convictions of ten
defendants in light of new requirements
that states provide lawyers for accused
persons who could not afford them. On
October 15, the National Cancer
Institute declared the anticancer drug
Krebiozen "ineffective." On October 16,
NASA secretly launched two satellites
designed to detect man-made nuclear
blasts in space. On October 19, South
Vietnam crushed a student attempt to
overthrow the Diem government. On
October 20, Jim Brown set a career rush-
ing mark of 8,390 yards. On October
25, the mayor of Dallas apologized to
Adlai Stevenson for insults Stevenson
received in Dallas on the 24th. On
October 27, Dr. Michael Debakey
reported having implanted the first artifi-
cial heart in a human patient. On
October 30, the IRS reported a record
$105.9 billion collected in 1963. On
November 1, South Vietnamese soldiers

Dad said, and since he'd shot Japs
at Guadalcanal, and my uncle
had garrotted Nazis with piano wire,
I hung on, stockpiling demerits,
praying to be discharged. Weekends—
shunned by my friends—I languished
in my room, or limped around
the house. "It's the marching,"
I told Mom. "My knees can't take it."
Monday of my sixteenth week, Mom
kept me home, and Tuesday, took me
to our family doctor, a good Quaker
named Haddock, who gave me
crutches and a note that said ROTC
was "too strenuous" for me. Wednesday,
I crutched straight to the Rot-see Room,
my note in a white envelope, my uniform
stuffed in a grocery bag. I handed both
to Captain Fleck. For the first time
since recruiting day, he looked at me.
The Army had "high hopes" for me,
he sighed as he read. And would
make "special arrangements" for me.
And would be "sorry to lose" me.
When I hung my head and said
nothing, he slashed his name across
my withdrawal form, and turned away
as if I were roadkill. I actually sang—
"Roll Over Beethoven"—under my breath
as I crutched back to the gym to face
the stinking towels and naked boys.
It would be seven years before, straight

violently overthrew the Diem government.
On November 2, President Diem was
found dead. Rebels claimed his death was
suicide. On November 3, Valentina
Tereshkova, the first woman in space,
married fellow cosmonaut Andrian
Nikolayev. On November 5, the Federal
Reserve Board raised the margin require-
ment for stock purchases from 50 to 70
percent. On November 6, a U.S. Court
of Appeals ruled that the Black Muslim
movement was not a religion, and not pro-
tected as such by the Constitution. On
November 7, the Soviets displayed four
"antimissle missles" in a military parade
through Red Square, and New York
Yankee Elston Howard became the first
Negro MVP from the American
League. On November 9, Texas voters
rejected a repeal of the poll tax. On
November 12, TASS announced the
arrest for espionage of the chairman of
Yale University's Department of Soviet
Studies. On November 14, AFL-CIO
President Meany denounced automation
as "a curse to society." On November 15,
Argentina canceled oil contracts
with U.S. firms as a first step toward
nationalizing the oil industry. On
November 18, despite protests from Arab
Catholics, the Vatican absolved Jews of
guilt for the death of Christ. On

off the college track team, I stood
in a line of hairy butts, and coughed
while an Army doctor felt my balls
to be sure they were good enough to lose
in Vietnam; but when I faced the scowling
major at the end, ROTC had taught me
what to do. Dr. Haddock's letter
detailed my knee problems, and threw in
asthma, plus a psoriasis he'd called
"a guaranteed 4-F." When Major growled,
"This girlie's got more damned
diseases than Carter has liver pills,"
and stamped my papers "Unfit
for Military Service," I gathered them,
and hung my head, and said nothing,
just limped tragically from the room,
and kept limping for two blocks
before I broke into a trot, then loped
along to "Purple Haze," my life snapping
like a clean white towel in my hands.

*November 22, President Kennedy was
killed in Dallas. Vice President Lyndon
Johnson was sworn in as president.
On November 24, Lee Harvey Oswald,
Kennedy's accused assassin, was shot
to death by Dallas nightclub owner
Jack Ruby. On November 26,
Congress declared a moratorium on parti-
san politics for a mourning period of thir-
ty days. On November 28, Cape
Canaveral, Florida was renamed Cape
Kennedy. On December 4, an American
Cancer Society study conclusively linked
cigarette smoking with early death, and
Pope Paul VI authorized use of the ver-
nacular in the Catholic mass and sacra-
ments. On December 11, Frank
Sinatra Jr., 19, was released unharmed
after his father paid kidnappers
$240,000 cash for him.*

Part II

Lost Lives

"I feel as if I've lost my life," a bald man said.
"In the sense that I misplaced it. How do I find it again?"
"Pay attention to particulars," the speaker said.

She was small, with long, gray hair. Two strands
of marble-sized white costume pearls offset
her black shirt, pants, and tennis shoes. I paid

attention to my seat's particulars—the curved
blond wood that creaked when I shifted my weight.
I paid attention to the podium—helmet shaped,

with a bent-microphone-feather; to the stagelight-
cauldrons dumping their bright soup; to the chairs
crouched by the speaker like a spider in two parts.

My feet would not stop fidgeting. I'd left work
early and sped here, listening to news about a bomb.
Two hundred people had lost their lives—

in the sense that they were dead—to terrorists
no one could have stopped, the commentators said;
we should expect more fathers vaporized at desks,

mothers guillotined by glass, children pulled bloody
from the day care womb. I hadn't paid attention
to the way I parked and hurried through the night

where two hundred absences still hung like smoke.
I hadn't paid attention to how gracefully my arms
swung by my sides, my legs pistoning me up

the concrete stairs to this "talk" in this Music Room.
Begging pardon, I squeezed past my neighbors' legs,
pushed (through their disapproval) out, and paid

attention to the moon, the ghosting clouds, the green
grass fingers gathering dew, the glittering concrete-
and-asphalt road that could take me anywhere.

The Age of Orange: A History Inferred from Sentences in the *Oxford English Dictionary*

—for Pattiann Rogers

In the year 1200, St. Dominic planted an orange
for the convent of St. Sabina. In the year 1201,
St. Sabina dug up the orange and planted St. Dominic,
and vice versa for the next two hundred years,
the Dark Age struggling, via the Tenebrous Age,
into the Gray Age, then torn out by the roots and yanked
back to Dark, until in 1399 an Italian hairstylist
named da Vunci, mixing blood with sulfur, created
the fashion craze that named the "Age of Orange."

The sun rose like an orange in those days,
and plopped like one back into the sea. The human
head was thought to be an orange—some sweeter
than others, more nectarous, but oranges still. To smile
was to "split one's orange"; to scowl, to "squeeze" it.
The heart was "orange-that-thumps." Lovemaking
was "sharing the orange." Rape was called "crushing
her orange." Treaties were sealed by a game
of "Toss the Orange." To "drop the orange" meant War.

About his so-called "Spanish town," Conquistador
Juan Cabeza de Caracol was called *El Pajaro Anaranjado,*
the "Orange Bird." He did not like to eat orange juice
out of a pewter spoon, or drink it either. The cold metal

taste at war with the sweet tang—he could take that,
but not the *p-yoo* sound. He loathed *goblets* too,
preferring his orange juice from a crystal *tureen,*
or hollow horse's hoof, or virgin's slipper or lips—
a girl with breasts like oranges and a general juiciness.

His daughter, Caracola, with her Favorite, both covered
with orange ribbons, often sashayed to the playhouse,
where they'd sit, stewing their prunes. This had
to be done secretly. Her father was creating orange-
seed shrapnel, and armor of dried orange skins.
"The town is a sea," he would rage; "the playhouse, a ship,
and the orange girls, powder-monkies." After, an orange
leaf was laid on every finger bowl. Caracola feared
to be convicted of Fruit Treason—condemned to War at Sea,

or forced to powder a monkey's face in an obscene
travesty of Woman's normal ritual, a Black Mass
of Makeup Application. But in time, along with fever-
in-the-blood, the prunal urge began to wane,
and she could scour the streets again, with the aid
of Fuller Brushmen who had started to appear.
The Age of Orange was losing steam, and after stops
in the Baroque and the Enlightenment, hissed to a halt
in the Age of Multicultural Disenchantment.

A defoliant that caused headaches, nerve damage, cancer,
and the birth of freaks was named spitefully "Agent Orange."
Parfait Amor, once made from bitter zest of orange,
spirit of rose, and cinnamon, had become whatever
could be scooped from the nearest ditch and sold,
in a blown glass bottle, for a king's ransom. Alas,
there were no kings. A new St. Dominic planted
another orange for a new convent of St. Sabina.
And so back to orange fizz and the ritual conference.

Rumpelstiltskin Convention

> Little knows my royal dame
> that Rumpelstiltskin is my name.
> —*The Brothers Grimm*

Circus Circus swarms with us: floors strewn

With straw, a spinning wheel in every room,

Gold lamé spilling from the slot machines.

Our name "makes us special," we say.

But no one calls us "dear Rumpy" or "sweet

Stiltskins." We don't marry—even each other;

Who worth having wants a Rumpelstiltskin?

At Caesar's Palace, Elvis imitators

Uh huh huh ecstatically. Long

John Silvers crutch across Treasure Island,

Squawking duets with their African Grays.

Sir Isaacs juggle apples at the MGM,

And reinvent the calculus.

The Luxor writhes with Cleopatras

And their snakes until bedtime, when the royal

Headdress and papyrus skirt slide off,

And nude women shower as themselves.

We can lose our nametags, but the name remains.

I drag mine with me like a dead Siamese twin,

Aching for the day—as the Queen teases,

"Is your name Doodad? Finiculi Finicula?

Pepto Bismol?"—I break, and scream,

"Rumpelstiltskin, bitch! You know it's Rumpelstiltskin!"

I'll throw her child, then, that I won fair and square—
The only thing that ever loved me—back
Into her pasty arms, and stamp so hard
One foot sinks deep into the dirt of this country
That "celebrates diversity." I'll grasp
The leg still free, and with one yank, tear
Myself like a wishbone limb from limb,
Thinking *Kevin*, thinking *Jimmy*, thinking *Bo*.

The Secret History of Rock & Roll

—for Stephen Dunn

Elvis Presley, Bo Diddley, Bill Haley & the Comets
were lies created on recording tape by the same Group
who made The Bomb, with the same motive:
rule the world. The Little Richard tunes

that made my five-year-old legs bounce and twitch,
and sent me skidding around the dinner table
screaming "Ooh my soul!" and "Woo!" were drugs
poured in my ears to make me despise Sunday School.

Jerry Lee Lewis's marriage to his 13-year-old cousin,
and Chuck Berry's violating the "Man Act"
were lies to make Rock seem more true. Buddy Holly,
Richie Valens, the Big Bopper died when their three

robots blew up in a thunderstorm. In 1962,
I bought a ten-dollar guitar, and squandered
homework time strumming "Little Deuce Coupe,"
dreaming of surfer girls. I joined a "Mersey"

band in '65, faked a British accent, and got swats
at school for past-the-collar hair. My parents' truth
was no match for the Beatles & Rolling Stones hoax,
the Kinks & Yardbirds & Zombies sham.

Vietnam was a staged backdrop for their songs.
Only the fact that every kid my age was equally
impaired let me squeeze into college, where my band,
Lethe, made me forget English, Physics, History,

as Cream, Led Zeppelin, Spirit, Hendrix, Sergeant
Pepper marched me toward burned draft cards
in a "purple haze." When, after Woodstock,
Dad threatened to hold me down and cut my hair,

I said "Try it," and left to play guitar full-time.
The Group's World War II masterminds
were dying out, but their successors created
Johnny Rotten, David Bowie, Kiss, and Queen,

while I fought to get my "sound" onto vinyl,
never dreaming that the record companies
who sent back encouraging *Nos,*
were mail drops just like those to Santa Claus.

Disco gave me a good long look at The Lie.
I quit my band, married, and got a job
teaching Psychology. The Yngwe Malmsteen
android made me pick my "ax" back up,

and relearn a few licks. Emotion roused
by ZZ Topp's "Can't Stop Rocking" caused
the fight that unmarried me in '92
and made me swear I'd quit the U and hit the road.

But sense prevailed. Now, though my feet still tap,
I see Rap, Hip Hop, Grunge, and Techno-Rock
for what they are. The decay preachers railed
against when "Elvis" shook goes on.

I barely know my country anymore.
The Group has won. But I've escaped. One kid
who lived for Rock has seen the light.
My brain was not my own. I renounce that boy.

Stegosaurus

For back plates, I use the chipped blue dinnerware
my wife left after our divorce; for tail spikes,
railroad nails swiped from a Texas historical site;
for skin, a chartreuse nylon tent used only once
because my wife and I had such a screaming fight,
a Yellowstone ranger made us leave.

Pumping my pedals, cranking my steering wheel,
I lumber into Accounting, and give free rides.
At night, I scatter muggers with my tail. "Next time
I see you without a job, I'll give you something to not
have a job about," I roar from the loudspeaker in my throat.
Next morning, they're all scanning the Classified.

My eyes, made out of cereal bowls, glow
with a blue, religious light. The bearded man slinking
out of The Pleasure Chest cradles his dildo
like a holy child. The bag lady dancing the twist
at Gabby's Chicken could be Mary Magdalene.
Cars slide up and down the freeways like rosary beads.

The L.A. *Times* profiles me, roaring of the need
for scorpions and spiders to be embraced as friends,
for summonses to be redeemable in ice cream,
kisses to be legal tender, doctor bills to be computed
in *Thank yous*. Fox offers me my own talk show.
Both parties plead with me to run for President.

I want to leap from my stego and squeal, "Surprise!"
But I don't dare. I lumber down congested streets,
letting people pat my nylon sides and stroke my corrugated
cardboard head. Do I feel my (ex)-wife's hand?
I whirl; she is lost in the crowd.
My microphone drops, shattering; I can't speak.

Just after midnight, the ropes moving my legs break.
Still, people pat me where I hunker in the street.
Cars growl behind me. Airplanes shriek.
Steam sways like ferns rising out of sewer grates.
Buildings loom like sandstone cliffs.
One day they will cover us all.

Tarantula

Time, from my burrow, was a string of beads,
Alternating black-and-cold, white-and-hot,
Before you came. I was one of a trillion

Living tips of the spider vine already
Thriving when your ancestors wriggled from
The surf. Then, one dawn—a rumbling

In the desert. A glow like the sun on a hot
Day. I started growing. My burrow
Was too small; I found a cave. I didn't mean

To kill the driver of that scurrying black
Ford. My web was spun, fangs
Bloody before I could think. Yes, I could

Think. My brain was growing with my body,
Senses heightening until I looked down
On your world like a god. I saw it all:

Your frantic phone calls, the screaming
Blonde with her tight shorts and pretty legs
That made the square-jawed hero accept

Her "wild stories" as the old sheriff barked,
"Talk sense!" To make him believe in me,
I sacrificed a farmer and his wife,

The way your old God used to do. I pitied
You the way He must have as you fled
The monsters you always create.

No wonder He died! Who could live
With such knowledge? Your National Guard
Were weak as ant larvae against me.

I found the square-jawed one the others
Followed because he was handsome, and placed
The word "electrocution" in his brain.

I didn't die the way you thought, trapped
With my eggs in that dark cave already
Grown too small for me. I led you there.

Watch for Deer

the sign commands me, and I do.
Day or night, dusk or dawn,
my head twists like a weathervane.

I watch for deer blending with pine trees
as I drive, hiding like cops behind billboards,
about to step out and be seen.

I watch for deer at work—
deer collating by the Xerox machine,
deer in the restroom, urinating daintily,

trying not to clatter their hooves
on the scrubbed tile floor.
I watch for deer on the freeway

in their Celicas with raised antler-roofs.
I watch for them in the cloud-animals
that graze the purple evening sky.

I watch others watching, too.
Children watch briefly, then return
to hooting, "You cheated! No fair!"

Teens watch when adults force
them to, then return
to watching one another's jeans.

Old people watch best, braced
for the moment when some elegant
buck or demure doe steps

from shadows, fixing them
in those brown eyes cartoonists love.
The chosen one trembles at first,

then, limbs grown light as air,
follows the deer into the forest
which is rising everywhere.

Cherubs

Women love them; so I say I love them too.
I toss them bread crumbs as if they're begging sparrows,
and squeeze out a grin when they flap by.

Like that of bees, their flight is aerodynamically
impossible. Still, they beat at my windows
like vampire bats, and swoop in front of my high beams.

I have to hose their dead off my windshield, and scrape
baby fat out of my headlights and chrome grill.
They're no good as guardians; when Denver Booth

kicked my butt in seventh grade, he kicked theirs too.
They've never granted me one wish, or warned before
the Market dove. They only hover like a swarm

of pudgy gnats. "You never go to church," they keen.
"You didn't write to Grandma; now she's dead."
(I should be grateful that, despite their statues, real ones

lack urinary tracts; I should be glad they're powered
by pure heavenly light.) Lose weight, I tell them.
Grow up and stop embarrassing me! I hoped

to be an intellectual Attila, driving insight's spear
through people's hearts, chilling their shiny toenails
blue. Fat chance, when cherubs spin like pink

planets around my head!   Fly into a black hole,
why don't you? Go make a Big Bang.
I wanted to be fearsome as a mafia Don—

dreadful as H-bombs and melanoma.
I never wanted to usher at the opera on my days off.
I never meant to own an antique store.

Munchausen's Syndrome

Named for the eighteenth century teller of tall tales, the syndrome's essential feature is the individual's plausible presentation of factitious physical symptoms to such a degree that he or she is able to obtain and sustain multiple hospitalizations.
—Diagnositic and Statistical Manual of Mental Disorders, *Third Edition*

I detail for the nurse my rectal bleeding,

the needles I feel wriggling through my lungs.

I tell the CNAs who push the gurneys

"Hurry!" as they ease me onto one,

and skate me to the examining room.

I guzzle down the smell of antiseptic

and adhesive spiced with necrosis,

while I amaze the doctor, telling how I lived

with the Amazon Su-Samaris until felled

by a liver parasite that plagues me still;

how, flying solo over the South Seas,

I crashed, and have suffered from *syncope*

and *hemoptysis* ever since. Subtlety's

my secret: slow striptease as opposed

to modern bare-it-all-and-spread. I tantalize

with intermittent fevers, roving pains,

until the doctors beg to give me what I want:

fasting and enemas, injections

and IVs before I'm wheeled into the theater
like royalty, the instruments like glowing
jewels, my flesh—cross-hatched

from other surgeries—eager to open
as the anaesthesiologist leans:
masked Daddy, whispering "Sweet dreams."

Gifts

He gives her a dozen red roses.
"Blood lilies," she says.
"Their breath will poison me.
But I forgive you," she says

and gives him a silk necktie.
"A speckled python," he says.
"It will strangle me.
But I forgive you," he says

and gives her a down comforter.
"A feather grave," she says.
"You want to tuck me under it.
But I forgive you," she says

and gives him a new Porsche.
"A fast wheelchair," he says.
"You want me helpless in it.
But I forgive you," he says,

and gives her a new house,
the kind she loves in magazines.
"A mausoleum," she says.
"We'll live happily ever after here."

Scarcity

Stop coming from Scarcity, and come from Abundance.
—*Ad in a New Age journal*

There aren't enough prizes here. There aren't enough
MacArthur Genius Fellowships to go around,
enough cheese sandwiches, lug nuts, or gruel.

White people here hate brown people, who hate
them back; white and brown people detest black people,
who detest them back, because there aren't enough

presidencies and bailiwicks and medical degrees,
enough waitress stations or dish-washerships.
If I work hard and get a Porsche or an A,

someone has to walk or get a D. People lucky
enough to have microscopes can see every
amoeba, every nematode fighting for food,

struggling for space. People lucky enough to have
vacations can see redwings flash crimson shoulders
to warn other birds away. They can hear elk

trumpeting, "This harem's mine. And I don't share."
There's no such thing as a free lunch in Scarcity.
If I want your roast beef sandwich, I must give you

my nachos and chocolate shake. We call it "Trade."
The scarcer something is, the more desirable.
Diamonds flash brighter than rhinestones because they're rare.

Even when there's plenty of some good thing, our people
multiply until it's scarce again. I've heard rumors
of Abundance, where everyone has lots of everything.

I'd go there, except I hear gunfire and bombs.
Except I hear, above the squeak of its contracting land mass
and shrinking perimeter, everybody screaming to get in.

Legacy

What can I leave you, children? Not my trained
flea, loyal sidekick all these years; the traitor's
run off with a cat. Not my alligator
shoes. Even the 'gator, barefoot, disdained
to take them. Not Mom's wisdom or pained
glare, or the conscience of a senator.
Not a whore's pyrite heart, an elevator's
moods, my early promise—unsustained.

My sense of purpose, which you should have had,
is lost. This room is such a mess, I can't
find anything, not even the Blue Funk
which served well when the good old days turned bad.
Forget them! These days are young and petulant,
do drugs, have unsafe sex, don't work, drive drunk.

"Octopus,"

Divers call their emergency air-source, since, when its hose is added
       to the three already
On the metal tank that humps a diver's back, the tank looks like a
       cephalopod—a quadropus,
Technically, but the guy who named it wasn't a linguist or the engineering
       type who coined
"Bouyancy Control Device," "Submersible Pressure Gauge," "Regulator—
       First and Second Stage";
He was the diver students are warned not to be: impulsive daredevil,
       willing to make a leap—
"That thing looks like an octopus!"—and let the dogpaddlers follow,
       wagging their heads.

I'll bet he was a Navy Seal: underwater saboteur, marvel of Yankee
       strength, ingenuity, lethal force,
Who dives to show old Ocean who's the boss. I'd love to be that kind of
       diver! But when Nature
Passed out gear, I got an extra-large Risk Assessment Device, a small
       Pain-Inhibiting Mechanism,
And a gigantic Fear of Jaws Factor, ensuring that I'd be the boy a future
       Seal's mom would want
Him to play with instead of the hoodlums he preferred, and a man who
       wears a seat belt, drives defensively,
Saves in CDs, not stocks, and delays everyone on the dive boat while I
       review Marine Biology

And triple-check my gear, straining to recall "Blonde [Bouyancy] Women
        [Weights] Really [Releases]
Are [Air] Fun [Final Okay]," though chance has dealt me a blonde "buddy"
        who could be great fun
If I were the Seal type who'd jump right in and steal her from her fiancé.
        I'd let her swim, enraptured
By Blue-Horned Whatsits, Bladder-Looking Fish, Menorah-of-the-Sea Coral,
        chartreuse Aunt Henrietta's Hats—
Then I'd grip her arm, give the finger-across-throat "out of air" sign and,
        refusing her octopus,
Make her "buddy-breathe," passing her mouthpiece back and forth: a life-
        sustaining kiss.

Trust

When I walk into a restaurant and order the trout almondine,
I have to trust that it is trout, and not dogfish or mudpuppy—
that my cream of mushroom appetizer won't be creamy
with earwax; my cafe au lait, not laced with phlegm.

When I step on the sidewalk, I have to trust that it will hold me,
that no bombs wait underneath the cracks (which cannot hurt
my mother's back), and that even in Los Angeles, no fissure
will gape and swallow me. Buying a new car, I have to trust

that, though the salesman may cheat me, he really does work
for the car company, and for my money will give me a real
car with engine, tires, working parts, and seats that won't crush
both my legs when I get in, or gush seawater, drowning me.

I must believe my tetanus booster isn't healthy tetanus germs,
or arsenic, or HIV, that my X-rays won't give me cancer,
that I won't catch anything incurable from the slumped patients
wheezing in the waiting room, or from the poor catastrophe

who stumbled out to die moments before I took the only empty chair.
Even the most paranoid howler in the rubber room has got to trust
that there *are* radio transmitters in his hair, that Martians beam
their dirty thoughts to him, and by knowing this, he can be saved.

Therefore, when I say "I love you," you don't have to do it now,
tomorrow, or next week; but someday before I stop saying it,
you have to trust that, though it could mean "I want to fuck you,"
or "I want to hurt you," or "I want you in my power totally,"

it more likely means "I want good things for you," or even
"I want to spend my life with you (although I know things change)."
And if you finally say it back, I have to trust you're not an IRS
agent out to disallow my writer's deductions—that you weren't

sent by the FBI to plant cocaine on me because of my seditious
poems—that almost no one reads my poems, so I can tell
the truth in them—that you're not the kind who wouldn't join
any club that would have you—that you're not plotting

to marry me, get bitchy and fat, then milk me dry—
and that together in this treacherous, bugged, mined, shifting
hall of mirrors, we can relax sometimes, let down our guard,
and live.

Prozac

It's transforming the world the way Leary said dropping acid,
Mahareshi said meditation, Christ said Christianity would.
Polly next door, bedridden since her husband's stroke,

laughs from her car, "It makes me tipsy, like champagne."
Clients in psychotherapy, after sweating years like miners
in the bowels of the unconscious, gulp their tabs and say they're cured.

Cartoons appear: Poe tells a raven, "Nice birdie."
Hitler, dancing the hora, shouts, "Master race, schmaster race."
Patrick Henry proclaims, "Give me liberty, or 20 milligrams."

Friends slide into the fold. My ex-wife calls to say "I can't believe it—
I see things your way!" This is more radical than microchips,
cloning, genetic engineering, virtual reality. Aggressor nations

may fall to Prozac bombs. People will still die, but who will care?
It will seem as strange to lament mortality as to wish people still shrieked
through surgery, made pumpernickel loaves from scratch,

dragged covered wagons over prairies full of Indians,
just to own a home. Teenagers, to rebel, will refuse drugs.
They'll return from dates at nine o'clock—still virgins—and scream

at their parents sprawled on the couch, giggling at car chases
in front of the boob tube. They'll run to their rooms
in despair, finish their homework, then write of their discovery

of pain. It gives such depth to life, they'll say, such gorgeous nuances: crimson, purple, emerald, pink. If everyone could feel this way, they think, it would transform the world.

The Function of Poetry

Poetry doesn't seem that functional . . .
—*engineering student*

It's to kick consciousness into higher
orbit, the way subatomic particles slam
into an electron dutifully circling
its nucleus and—wow!—it makes
two quantum leaps and spurts
blue light.

        It's to shock us into trance,
the way a preacher, after soothing
the sick with hymns about God's
golden throne, screams "HEAL!"
and pounds a palm into the forehead
of a man who swoons into the arms
of deacons hovering like cherubim,
and wakes, cured of cancer
for a day,

        or the way a hypnotist
drones about the heat, her son's soccer,
the belly-dancing candle flame,
then s l o w s   h e r   v o i c e
and while your brain is startled,
wondering what to do, clamps a strong
hand on your shoulder, shoves you
into a soft chair, and whispers,
"Everything is possible. Deep sleep."

Byron, Keats, and Shelley

Decide to temper Romantic *Sturm und Drang* with comedy.
          Keats shaves his head;
               Shelley frizzes out his hair;
Byron submits to a bowl cut.

          My heart aches, and a drowsy numbness pains
               My sense, as though of hemlock I had drunk,
Keats sighs, his head stuck in a cannon.

          Eternal Spirit of the chainless Mind!
               Brightest in dungeons, Liberty!
Byron shouts, and lights the fuse.

O wild West Wind, thou breath of Autumn's being,
          Thou, from whose unseen presence the leaves dead
               Are driven, like ghosts from an enchanter fleeing,
Shelley booms, and drops a cannonball on Byron's toe.

          Exiled to the continent, they write their famous
               Trilogy: *Idiots Deluxe, Half-Wits Holiday,*
And their masterpiece, *Mummies Dummies,*

          In which Byron plays Ozymandias embalmed,
               And Keats gets his nose slammed in a sarcophagus,
Runs head-first into a sphynx, and staggers

Around rubbing his pate as Shelley mugs beside

    The shattered sphynx and states, *Round the decay*

        Of that colossal wreck, boundless and bare,

The lone and level sands stretch far away . . .

    Then the curtain falls on his head.

        The trio tours Paris, Berlin, Vienna, Prague—

Tuba players blowing wigs off heads-of-state;

    Dogcatchers wrapped in their own nets;

        Waiters flinging cream pies,

Dumping cauldrons of hot soup in courtly laps

Until they die, too young, careening

    Into immortality covered with flour, squealing,

        Drainpipes on their heads—which explains why

For many years, the greatest poems

    In English have all ended *Nyuk, nyuk, nyuk,*

        And why, reading *She walks in beauty like the night . . .*

We are as clouds that veil the midnight moon . . .

    Season of mist and mellow fruitfulness . . .

        You may feel ghostly pliers tweak your nose,

And ghostly fingers poke the tear ducts in both eyes.

Poem on My Anniversary

She's fifteen, struggling to hold her schoolbooks
as she digs in her purse for exact bus fare:
two quarters and one dime that squirms away
as the folding yellow door hisses shut.

She jumps back as the bus pulls out, and feels
herself unwrapped like a burrito, spun
like a carpet unrolling, the bus charging off
flying the jade-and-purple banner of her skirt.

That morning she couldn't find her blue
Monday panties; now the world sees pink
Saturday as she sprints in tears to Macy's,
and jumps into the first skirt on the rack.

A philosopher might say, "Our culture wraps us
in its fears," or "Fate strips away our prized
possessions." A novelist could dress up
the girl's story with romance—say that Hollywood

discovered her that day; that she met her future
husband, instead of waiting sixteen years
for me. But I can see her breathless
dash—how everyone on Beverly Drive stares

as if spring sun has broken through November gray—
how their burdens, for an instant, are turned light
as styrofoam, and they wake to their lives, grateful,
as I wake to mine today

Part III

Someone Else's Good News

Even as I say, "That's fantastic!
I'm glad for you," my hand quivers, my mood
Conks out, flaming, at 30,000 feet.
What is the sound of "overjoyed," and how
Convey it, as if what is good for friends
Is good for me—as if my own crippled
Hopes aren't leaping off gurneys, flopping
Out of wheelchairs screaming, "Shit! Shit! Why
Wasn't it me?!" Sheepish good sport, bloody-
Nosed loser shaking the champion's hand,
Poor jilted chump who sends a wedding gift
And sings "Take good care of my baby,"
I wince to hear how winner Joan almost
Skipped the contest I've entered faithfully
For twenty years, how winner John rang
The wrong doorbell and blundered into the woman
I've spent thousands on dating services
And flirting seminars trying to find.
I feel mean, treacherous, small: fighting
Not to think "Get cancer," "Die in a car wreck,"
"Be burned alive with your pisshead cheerful
Wife and noisy, overindulged kids."
Trophy trout leaping on every line
But mine, I crash upstream, downstream, cursed
By everyone whose cast I cross, whose hole
I hog—all dignity lost, all pretense gone.
I foam with envy as if I'm a salted snail.
Acid in my eyes: the excitement

Of the fortunate, the grin (politely restrained)
That still says *I've done it! I've arrived!*
While for me it's *Oh God no,* back
To page one, back to the empty canvas, back
To the old job, back to the hands above
The keyboard, paralyzed, not knowing how
To start again. I wave as friends' yachts leave
The dock, straining to hoist the corners
Of my mouth, although the little Atlases
Supporting them have gulped bad oysters, and
Just want to lie down, just want to throw up.

Photo Titled "Birth"

The newborn's eyes squint miserably in the light,
sparse hair sopping, mouth a deep gouge of disgust.
All philosophy starts here. Before the lungs
can power the first scream, the face proclaims, "Oh shit,

what's this?"—baby Buddha wakened to life's suffering,
baby Adolph up to his moustache in *Mein Kampf*.
Snaking from his belly, past his twig-penis,
down into the thatch between Momma's thighs,

the boy's wrinkled umbilicus shrinks already
from the knife, withers, collapses: his last link
to that warm dark where he drifted, consciousness
dawning as in the Hindu creation. ("This am I,"

thinks Brahma, and—his ego born—becomes
afraid.) Already memory evaporates
into the clouds of glory Wordsworth pictured trailing
souls to earth—a fading star-path, faint skywriting

leading back beyond the cross and Bodhi tree
to heaven, nirvana, oblivion,
toward which the baby's head struggles to lift.
Toward which his body, spanked alive, already falls.

Lampwick

Outside, boys plink slingshots, blat trumpets,
chase cats and sad-eyed donkeys down
Pleasure Island streets paved with cookies,
lined with doughnut-trees—no lima bean or stalk
of broccoli in sight.

                    Inside the Pool Hall,
Lampwick—red-haired little thug—chomps a stogie
and shows Pinocchio his shot-behind-the-back.
Mid-stroke, he stops. Long ears pop
out of his head. His tailbone grows. And grows.
His feet harden to hooves. His head lengthens,
voice gouged and scraped into a hoarse *Eee haw!*

The audience snickers in the popcorn-scented dark.
But when snarling goons drag Lampie off
to the slave ship (green swell's hat still cocked
on his donkey head), and he starts to bawl,
Eee haw, eee haw! I want my mother!—kicking
and thrashing like a man gut-shot, a convict
dragged to the electric chair—all laughter stops.

No bad boys thunder through the aisles,
stomp Coke cups, frisbee Necco wafers at the screen.
As children chew this nightmare-fodder,
we parents shrink in our jeans.
                              Forgetting
Pinocchio, whose journey to become a real boy
is only sidetracked temporarily by ass ears
and a tail, we feel the chains that bind us upright
in our velvet seats, the oars we mostly manage
to forget blistering our hands, the lash
bloodying our backs, the same slavemasters
who bought Lampie howling, "Row!"

Coach Class Seats

Each has a foot-square paper napkin stuck
to the headrest: a bow to budget travelers' sensibilities.
Too bad each square evokes a paper toilet seat:
a 747 full of people shuffling in, then settling down to reek.

At least my hair won't pick up grease
from God-knows-whom. At least I won't be colonized
by roaming lice, or forced to lie, in effect, cheek-to-cheek
with a stranger (though his brain contains the same serotonin,

dopamine, and endorphins as mine, that mediate
the same trembling at takeoff, same intake of breath,
same slow relaxing of the hands on the armrests
as the plane climbs and the earth opens its green Atlas below).

No other head has ever been here, the squares state.
This experience is fresh, reserved for you.
The waiter changing the tablecloth before seating new
lovebirds where you've just proposed—

the nurse tearing a length of paper from the doctor's
table on which you bled and writhed—no,
you're not interchangeable, these gestures say. The way
that two-pound brookie sipped your Wooly Bugger,

then wrapped your line around a jutting root has never
in fishing history occurred before today.
Your fingerprints: unique as snowflakes. Your lover's
kiss: nonpareil. You were the first, stepping onto your lanai

in Kona, ever to say, "Whoa, honey, look at that view!"
How cheap the thrill if everybody felt that way.
Of course they don't, these napkins say. In all the miles
this plane will fly, there'll never be a passenger to rival you.

Confidence

Every politico exudes it, even in the "candid" shots.
Even if he got two votes out of a googol,
and cast both himself. Even if he's been indicted
for making Earth, at gunpoint, shed its atmosphere—
still he beams on the front page, about to scream
"Oh, haw haw haw!" and slap his thigh,
self-satisfied as Yahweh on the seventh day.

All polls on what's sexy put confidence on top,
along with a nice ass and megabucks.
"I'm confident of one thing: failure,"
losers whine in my Get More Stuff seminars.
"Fake it till you make it," I roar. *Picture
an eagle diving on a dove.* Force a smile
when you're depressed. Your brain will believe

your lips, and decide things aren't so bad.
Picture a river glittering in summer sun.
Winners excel at self-deception.
Picture pot-bellied black bass inhaling frogs.
How far do you think boxers get who say,
"My opponent's faster, stronger, hits harder
than me. I'll go in two"? Better to proclaim

yourself the New "Floats like a Butterfly,
Stings like a Bee." Better to picture
a tsunami shrugging toward a helpless shore.
"Even if you forget the chords," I told myself
before concerts, "you can fool 'em with feedback
and flashy hands." Only once did I let myself
consider, on stage, "I could forget everything."

Presto—my mind was washed clean as a water slide.
The girls waving their room keys vanished.
My testosterone plunged to pre-puberty levels,
turning me back into the bumpkin I was
before I picked up a guitar and stepped onstage
with metal braces on my arms to stop the shaking,
and a big fake grin.

George

His name is *Jorge*, but he lets the man he works for
call him George, and runs to do his bidding,
even when the hammering Anglo syllables don't

drive much meaning home. With his blue Dodger cap
and white surgeon's mask, he scrapes the flaking
brown paint off my walls, perched on a plank

that trampolines, stretched between ladders, twenty feet
above the ground. "Sorry *por* noise," he says
as his tinny radio blats the oompah bass and sour

trumpets of station K-Buena! "When you suffer,
I suffer; when you weep, I weep," the tenor sobs
in Spanish. "It's so sad that Margarita cries."

Scrunched in the crawlspace, parting cobwebs,
pushing wires and plastic pipe up to his boss
who stands in clean dress pants in my kitchen,

George doesn't cry, though he has no HMO
to heal a spider-bite or break a fall—no worker's
comp and, most likely, no green card.

He eats cold tortillas for lunch, washed down
with water from my hose. Gangbangers shot
his brother in Pacoima, where George lives with "God

knows how many others," his boss says.
"Beats Guatemala, or he wouldn't be here."
It must be true. Still George tongue-ties me,

my *Español* shakier than his *Inglés.* I'm awkward
in my own house (that must seem palacial),
lounging in sweatpants and slippers, tapping

my computer as George sweats and strains.
He stares at my wife as if she's the blessed Virgin.
He unnerves her, and unmans me as valets do,

opening my car door. As bellhops do,
lugging my bags. I should be changing my own
rusty pipes, scraping my own paint, balancing

beside George on his plank. I don't know how
to deal with George in a democracy where citizens
won't do his work for his wages, or if they do,

toil sullenly—not like George, who sings:
honest, smiling George, who shares his name
with the Father of this country. Without George,

our lawns would brown and die, we'd eat on dirty
dishes, live in slums like the one he returns to
after changing his clothes in my garage, folding

his blue work shirt and overalls, easing on
the same worn slacks and flowered button-down,
combing his wet hair with his hands.

A month after he's gone, I find in my garage
a flyer from Hermana Maria, promising to cure
sickness, return lovers who stray, change

bad luck, ease pain in the legs, back,
stomach, head—drive out demons if need be.
Ella le mostrará la luz de Dios

y le devolverá la suerte, la salud,
y la felicidad. Con Dios, todo es posible.
Everything is possible with God.

Mother Asleep

The cat on her lap leads the way:
a black wheel rolling into dreams,
powered by the motor of its purr.

Her children chat, fear softening
their focus on her arms dwindling
toward bone, her wispy gray

hair with pink scalp burning through,
her cane—a third leg, thin
as the two which braid each other

by the heater flickering at her feet.
While her son rails at the economy,
she cartwheels off the high dive

at Ralph's Wharf, where real steam
paddle-wheelers used to dock.
Ringed by Feosol, Cytotex, Lanoxin—

incantations meant to hold Death back—
she's The Happy Flapper
in her freshman play, *Dixie Blackbirds.*

"Are you asleep?" her daughter asks.
Her eyelids creak, heavy as garage doors.
Someday soon she'll try to wake

and feel Death's lips cover her eyes,
Death's hand, scented with lilac, smooth
the last wrinkle of breath. But now

she answers, "No, Honey, I'm here . . ."
before her eyelids drop, and she becomes
Lady Constance, in love with a gypsy

(Vernon Needles in real life);
she becomes the Soul of Dance, spinning
through her favorite play, *The Merry Whirl.*

At Summer's End

I rise at dawn, and stumble up steep, crumbling
Rock to sit on a downed tree and lock
This morning in my mind: this mountain grooved
And channeled by spring runoff, poppies dancing
Like tethered butterflies as wind brushes
The deep harps of the trees. As a boy,

I played in woods like these, stalking the green,
Trilling warblers and rosy grosbeaks
That flocked to Houston, fleeing Canadian snow.
I notched my bb gun for every one I dropped,
And hung their wings above my bed to hover
With my dreams. Where, today, high-rise

No Pun

Condos block the sky, I netted monarchs
And red admirals; I tracked a fox
One whole Saturday, barely seeing the tall
Loblolly pines, they were so common, the stands
Of sweetgum and post oak where jays rasped
Just as they do here, while far away,

Bulldozers out-grumble the wind. Overnight,
I'm forty, near divorce, joints stiff
In morning chill, bald spot spreading like a meadow
In the trees. My bold resolves scatter
Like quail—so many so fast, I can't bring
Down even one. I zip my coat and stumble

Uphill over ground studded with stone,
Pitted with holes where chipmunks curl, still sleeping
In the earth's warm pouch. Decay surrounds me—
Ice-cracked rocks, sun-withered flowers,
Pine-needle peat, brown boulder-faces pondering
The mountain's end. Sage-mist rises.

Snow-scoured tree stumps twist and bend: the seasons'
Swirl sculpted in wood. My house in town
Keeps seasons out. Nothing gets inside
To heal me. Nothing makes me proud to join
The mountains' dance of change, their jagged, dwindling
Peaks vaulting across the sky. Here,

In a patch of dried asters, a butterfly
Blue as a chip of morning clings, waiting
For sun, which moves toward us—a slow avalanche
Of light—as I turn and, hand-in-hand
With gravity, start my long, stumbling
Dance downhill.

Losing My Hair

How can I walk outside without its springs
to bounce the sun back from my face?
How can I take my blind mother to church
and be seen as her life's potent continuation,
if hair stops doing copper pushups on my head?

How can I survive beautiful girls' eyes
with no curls crackling, "I'm full of fire for you!"
How can I not, at work, seem foolish, middle-
aged (must middle age always seem foolish?)
if no Birds of Promise nest above my brain?

Soft roof of the body's mansion—sleek
fur hat—pine-needled carpet covering
my bright ideas—protein extrusions,
helping me build happy times—
how can I order a Big Mac and feel kin

to the checkout girl, and not the dour drudge
with his name tag: Hank Skelley, Manager?
How can I start my car with a boyish
wrist flick? How can I fly coach class
to Denver, not mistaken for a mortal

who, if his plane crashed, could die?
Bring me potions, grafts, weavings, wigs,
gene therapy! How else can I get back
my seat in seventh grade? How else can I
hunt Easter Eggs, rejoin the Pee Wee League,

claim my half-price movie tickets,
my child's plate? Crown, miter, headdress
of youthful office, what should I do?
My head's a planet with failing gravity.
One by one its people fall into the sky.

It's Good That Old People Get Crotchety

It's good that they complain and snap and scold.
It's good they take all day to cross the street,
glaring, holding up their hands like traffic cops.

It's good they confuse us with cousins we despised.
It's good they stink of mold and slops, and their mouths gape,
black-toothed and snoring, when they sleep.

It's lucky they fall out of bed and break their hips
at 2 A.M. and must be driven to Emergency
when we have the flu. It's fortunate they're shunted

house to house like heirloom trolls—relatives vying
to create the most convincing reasons why
they can't take the oldster, although they'd love to.

It's good each morning we're afraid to find them
dead, and hope we do. It's good they bawl—
"I'm such a burden," "After all I've done for you,"

"Nobody wants me!"—and every word is true.
It's a godsend they answer the phone,
"take" messages they don't write down,

and yell, "They've chained me to the bed!"
It's fortunate that who they were sometimes floats
above their heads, then disappears,

and it's like watching Dad devolve into The Thing.
It's good even the "Home" we finally put them in
instead of buying a car that runs, fixing our roof

that leaks—the Home that will haul us to the Poor
House in a year—can't control their tantrums any more
than we can. So it's good they curse, and shriek

like birds, and won't stop fussing with their shit.
It's fortunate the jowly minister drops by,
spends a minute with his parishoner, and an hour

proselytizing us. It's good that, at the grocery store,
we lose our appetite, passing the Depends.
It's good we've cried so much, grief has become a bore.

It's good that every atom in those ancient bodies roars,
"I need," until we scream, "Oh God, just die!"
How else could we stand to let them go?

Love Poetry

Most people think it's what all poetry is—
that, or incomprehensible, which love is too.
But wonderful. Enough to make you swim
the Hellespont—or try. Enough to make
you drink poison, or shoot yourself to warn
your lover of a trap. Forget the cynics
who call you "codependent." What do they know
about love? It's better than being President.
Better than discovering a cure for Death,
your face on stamps from every country
in the world. Better than eating anything
you want and not gaining an ounce—
getting more physically fit with every Devilish
Mocha Cheesecake Delight. Look at pop songs,
movies, and books—so many people burning
calories in love's praise. Don't tell me
they "protest too much." All cynics are casualties
of love. They start hopeful as anyone,
but instead of strawberry crepes on Sunday morning,
they get a spider sandwich. Instead of hot oil
massages, they get drubbed with baseball bats.
Instead of all-expense-paid lives in Bora Bora,
they get the Gulag Archipelago.
                              Forget them.
See that couple ditching school? See how
she grips his arm at the elbow? See how they stop
on the sidewalk in front of the whole passing
adult world, and kiss? *French* kiss! See how

he kneads her ass?—not only without shame,
with pride. Look how proud they are of each other
as they resume walking, love tinting the air
around them like a big red heart. That isn't pap; ~ipple
that's poetry. Even if she gets pregnant that day,
and wrecks her life. Even if her father makes her
get an abortion and dump the guy. Even if
he finds a new girlfriend and flaunts her,
while his dream to be a rock star shrinks to a vow
to fish a lot, then dwindles to dust under his bed.
Even if she marries a cop who beats her,
and punches three kids into her before she's 20.
Even if the boy—now more or less a man—
sees her one day shopping at Ralph's, and doesn't
know her, she looks so sad and old. Even if
that girl was you, that boy was me. Even so.

Identifying with the Buddha

We forget, praising his lotus feet, that he named his son Rahula:
    "Fetter" or "Impediment."
This would seem cruel from anyone not vanquishing the fires of
    Lust, Hate, and Delusion—
especially when *his* parents named him Siddhartha: "Whose Aim
    Is Accomplished."

We fault others for naming children Ima Hogg, Ben Dover, Isabel
    Ringing,
knowing that Queen Latifah or Majestyk Magnyfycent will more likely
    shine than Debit, Ordure, Angina.
Consider John Graves the mortician; Fred Carie, the dentist; Lydia
    Spies, the paranoid—

yet "Rahula" is seen as just and wise, as is the fact that, 29, Siddhartha
    abandoned his wife and Impediment.
My grandad did that, and his name became a curse. Since no one calls
    Siddhartha *selfish, mean, a deadbeat dad,*
why badmouth me for naming St. Luke's pastor "Bore," my rich
    maiden aunt "Windfall,"

my demented mom "Millstone"? Her given name was much plainer
    than Mahamaya—
Mary Sue—and before my birth she didn't dream a silver elephant
    entered through her side,
as Siddhartha's mother did; still, at eight pounds five ounces, I felt
    like an elephant, she said.

After three miscarriages, my mother dreamed of holding a healthy child,
    and didn't care
if it grew up to enumerate the Four Noble Truths and reach nirvana,
    or became a shoeshine boy.
She didn't fall prostrate, but she worshipped me, instilling the sense
    of lovability

that lets me be, sometimes, a mean son-of-a-bitch. Hey, you monks
    with tinkling bells,
orange robes, shaved heads—why not sculpt stone statues of me?
    Why not build gold temples to me,
and carve wooden figures of me whose stomach (kept flat with situps
    and crunches) you rub for luck?

Why not revere me, and everyone with enough guts to call a fetter
    a fetter, enough spunk
to boot a Pekingese—yapping like Mara the Devil—when its owner's
    back is turned?
Siddhartha mortified the flesh until he looked like Uncle Rictus
    on *Tales from the Crypt*,

but didn't reach enlightenment until he ate well-balanced meals,
    and kicked back
in the shade of a Bo tree. I say it's trying to be so good, wise, pure,
    and self-denying
that's the real *rahula*. I say attachment to our virtuous suffering
    keeps us chipping teeth on,

bloodying wrists and ankles against, howling prayers and praises
    to our chains.
I say forget the old Buddha and follow me, or if not me, then
    the Pierces from Pacoima—
Dick and Patti—who work as a bus driver and grocery checker
    respectively,

drink too much, have put on weight, bicker about money and sex,
    but managed,
when Patti had twins—red, wrinkled, squalling bulletheads—
    to name one Celeste,
"heavenly," and the other David, "beloved."

Chapel in the Pines

It looks like an observatory: a white dome,
mid-L.A., flanked by one spindly conifer.
I'm here to sign permission forms that let
a sister-chapel in Rochester burn my mom.
I have to sign because "Cremation is so
final," *Tammy* said over the phone.
"Like death," I said—no, only thought it.
I do say "Nice catacombs," to break the silence

as Tammy leads me between walnut pews
into a stairwell lined with brass name plaques
and small brass vases. "We're a columbarium,"
she says. Some of the vases hold flowers—
red, yellow, purple; roses, lilies, daisies,
but no columbines that I can see as the rowed
names of the dead follow us down. "Sit, Cerberus,"
I say (or think) as we go deeper, then pass

through a door into an ordinary office: desk,
computer, swivel-chairs. Tammy hands me
a pamphlet, then slips off "to do your paperwork."
I read how the body that bore me will char
three hours at two thousand degrees before
the ash is crushed to "uniform consistency."
The willies attending that phrase drive me
into the next room, where I whistle "Does

Your Chewing Gum Lose It's Flavor on the Bed-
Post Overnight," and dance what I remember
of the Hokie Pokie. "A little life for you,"
I tell the ashes, consistent behind their plaques.
Hearing the swish of Tammy's skirt, I dart
back just ahead of her. "Sorry for the trouble,"
she says after I've signed. "If you believe we rise
from the dead physically, burning's not good."

"If God can raise the goo out of a grave,
he can raises ashes. Just add water,"
I definitely say, then "Sorry," as Tammy leads me
up what English calls a "flight" of stairs.
Clutching my copy of the form that consigns
my mom to flames—in the full health of my body,
as my cells burn sugar and oxygen to power
my leg muscles—light as Orpheus, I rise.

Inheritance

Even in wedding pictures, Mom and Dad
Looked like good Methodists, celibate
As saints. Then today, tasting the salt tang

Of your neck, breathing your scent of musk
And clover, the truth hits: When I change
A tire, thump a melon, fret over a check

Lost in the mail, I notice my parents in me;
Why not when squeezing breasts or kissing
Thighs? And you had parents, present too

As you kiss me. Our parents had them;
So did theirs, and theirs, who kissed, squeezed,
Gasped some version of "Yes, baby, yes!"

As your legs open and I enter you,
My mother opens for my dad to create me;
Your dad enters your mom; she enters him;

Their parents join the celebration stretching back
To when the first cell split, and both halves
Oozed away feeling *so good*—trilobite

And gorgosaurus, glyptodont, smilodon,
Archaeopteryx, all in our seething primordial
Bed out of which Mom and Dad rise,

Kiss, whisper, "Honey, that was great,"
Laugh like we do, and giddy as newlyweds,
Walk arm-in-arm inside us, out into the sun

Under the trees which breathe in carbon
Dioxide and breathe out oxygen, O_2:
Atoms forever coupling in the shameless air.

Liver

Largest gland in the human body, three-pounds-plus of spongy red-
brown meat
Shaped like a slug, or a fat, finless seal lodged in the abdomen's upper
right quadrant,
Canopied by diaphragm, nudging stomach and guts—you taste so foul
when cooked,
So musty and rotten, who would guess that you provide protein, vitamins
A, D, E, and B-complex,
Copper and iron? Who would guess the wealth of your accomplishments:
blood filter,
Storehouse for energy, aid to digestion, producer of antibodies, self-
regenerator.
Doctors hacked out three-fourths of my friend Ken's liver in Hamburg,
but it grew back.
Surgeons routinely take a chunk from an adult's liver and transplant it
to a child.
The adult's liver grows back to its full size; the child's new liver grows
as the child does.
Only vertebrates have livers. (Does this mean you house the soul?)
No wonder
Ancients centered emotions in you—so much larger than the heart, more
sanguine and substantial
Than the brain. No wonder, to Crow Indians, mountain man Jeremiah
"Liver-Eatin'" Johnson
Was more powerful than if he'd been merely "Heart-Eatin'," "Lung-
Eatin'," "Brain-Eatin'" Johnson.

Benedictions on the way blood percolates through you, Liver, en route
from the intestines to the heart.

Benedictions on the way you neutralize food additives, drugs, poisons,
        germs, excess sex hormones (too much of a good thing).

Benedictions on the way you store sugar as glycogen until it's needed,
        then reconvert it to sugar for energy.

Benedictions on the way you boost the blood with *albumin* (that keeps
        plasma from seeping

Through blood vessel walls), *fibrinogen* and *prothrombin* (that help
        blood clot),

Heparin (that stops blood from clotting when it shouldn't), *globulin*
        (that fights infections).

Benedictions on the way you convert ammonia to *urea*, discharged in
        urine.

Benedictions on your production of bile: green liquid that, despite
        medieval lies,

Improves the disposition, helping to break up globs of fat so that
        intestinal

Enzymes can change them into glycerol and fatty acids the body can
        use.

When red blood cells are destroyed in the bone marrow and spleen,
        and their hemoglobin

Dumped back in the blood, bless you, Liver, for taking this crimson
        dye and changing it

Into the folksily named red *bilirubin* and green *biliverdin* that flow
        with the bile

To the intestines, giving feces the brown color that warns our shoes
        away.

Astonishing, Liver, how you begin as a vestigal yolk sac.
        Astonishing,

How a net of blood vessels, the *vitelline vessels*, develops in the
        yolk sac's wall.

How the *umbilical vessels* develop to bring nourishment from the
> uterus.
How both sets of vessels link behind the heart, and enter in like
> lovers holding hands.
How at their junction, capillaries create the *septum transversum.*
> How cells detach
From the "liver bay" in the gut, and the *mesothelium* that lines the
> body cavity,
Then migrate to the *septum transversum*, surround the capillaries,
> and become liver cells.
How each of the liver's four lobes is made of multisided lobules—
> 50,000 to 100,000 per adult liver.
How each lobule is a central vein surrounded by bundles or sheets
> of liver cells.
How *sinusoid* cavities separate the cells, making the liver spongy,
> helping it hold blood.
How the *sinusoids* drain into central veins, which join to form the
> *hepatic vein*, from which blood leaves the liver.
How the mature liver is a labyrinth of crooked hallways and long,
> thin, crooked rooms.

Forgive me, Liver, for the swill I've pumped through you. Please
> keep doing your fantastic work,
Dear red-brown friend. I'm so afraid of hepatitis, that inflames you
> and could kill me.
I'm so afraid of cirrhosis, that turns you into yellow scar tissue,
> making you contract and fail.
I'm so afraid of cancer that chews you from the inside out, and jaundice,
> when the blood

Contains too much *bilirubin,* causing yellowing of the skin and eyes,
        warning
Of worse trouble to come. I'm so afraid of dysentery, histoplasmosis,
        t.b., and syphilis
That start elsewhere but take you over, Liver, the way kudzu has
        overrun the South.

You do much more for me every day than the Mayor. I think I should
        call you The Honorable Liver.
You do much more for me than the Governor. Liver for Governor.
        Liver for President—no, King!
I'd say "Liver for God," except you may already be. Our Liver, who art
        in heaven. Hail Liver, full of grace.
Organ of life, playing better than Bach the toccatas and fugues of good
        health and vitality,
Organ whose name contains the injunction "Live!"—O Liver, great One-
        Who-Lives, so we can too.

Descent

—for Erik Byron

Let
there be
amino acids,
and there were: a slop
of molecules in ancient seas,
building cell walls to preserve their
identities, dividing, replicating, starting
to diversify, one growing oars, one rotors, one
a wiry tail, lumping into clusters—cyanobacteria, sea
worms, medusae, trilobites, lobe-finned fish dragging onto
land, becoming thrinaxodon, protoceratops, growing larger—
diplodocus, gorgosaurus—dying out—apatosaurus, tyrannosaurus—
mammals evolving from shrew-like deltatheridium into hyenadon, eohippus,
mammoth, saber-tooth, dire wolf, australopithecus rising on two feet, homo erectus
tramping from Africa into Europe and Asia, thriving like a weed that will grow anywhere—
jungle, desert, snow-pack—the genetic rivers flowing downhill now: a husband's skull crushed
in the Alps, a Tartar raping a green-eyed girl who dies in childbirth, whose daughter falls in
love with a Viking who takes her to Istanbul, a Celt who marries a Saxon, a weaver
who abducts the daughter of a witch, a son who steals his father's gold, a girl
who loses one eye leaping from a tree, dozens who die of smallpox,
cholera, black plague, a knight, a prostitute, thieves, carpenters,
farmers, poachers, blacksmiths, seamstresses, peddlers of
odds and ends, an Irishman who sells his family into
servitude, a Limey who jumps ship in New York,
Jews who flee Hungary, a midwife, an X-ray
machine repairman, a psychologist,
a writer, all flowing down,
converging on the great
delta, the point
of all this:
you.